You Are Part Of An Epic Team

www.ingramcontent.com/pod-product-compliance
Lightning Source LLC
Chambersburg PA
CBHW070433220526
45466CB00004B/1652
* 9 7 8 1 6 6 0 8 5 7 9 9 9 *